The United Nations

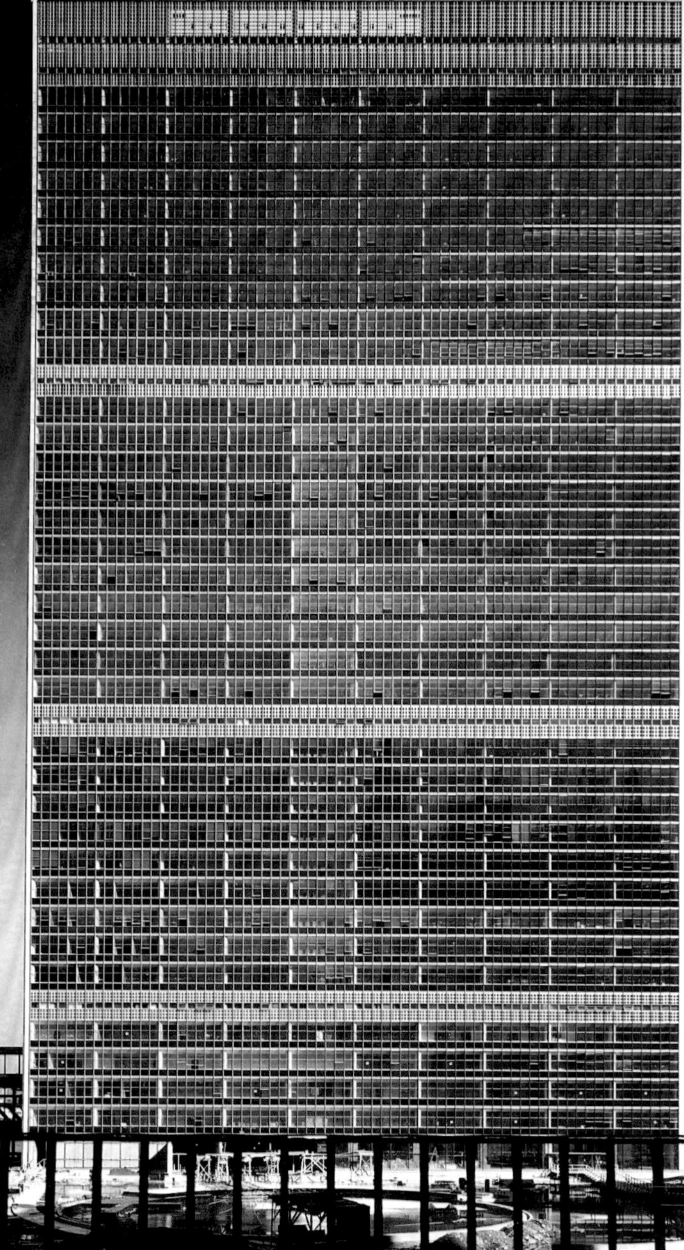

The United Nations

Photographs by Ezra Stoller

Introduction by Jane C. Loeffler

Princeton Architectural Press • New York

The BUILDING BLOCKS series presents the masterworks of modern architecture through the iconic images of acclaimed architectural photographer Ezra Stoller.

ADDITIONAL TITLES IN THE SERIES

The Chapel at Ronchamp
Fallingwater
The Salk Institute
The Seagram Building
Taliesin West
The TWA Terminal
The Yale Art + Architecture Building

Contents

Preface VII

Introduction 1

Plates 15

Drawings & Plans 91

Key to Images 94

Preface

Ezra Stoller

IN THE 1930S I was a student at the New York University School of
Architecture, which, for part of that time, was located on Forty-third
Street near Second Avenue. East of the school, along the river, were
the city's slaughterhouses. The animals were brought up the East
River by barge, and then driven along the street to the abattoirs, led
by the Judas goat. When the wind blew from the East, the odor
was…noticeable. This was the site that eventually became home to
the United Nations.

When the UN was being built my studio was on Thirty-seventh
Street between First and Second avenues, so I was ideally situated to
document what promised to be the most important governmental
complex on earth. My earliest commission, for *Architectural Forum*,
was to do a few photographs of the Secretariat Building while it was
under construction. But I was determined to record the project fully,
and since it was close to my shop I was able to spend a lot of my own
time doing just that.

I photographed the UN numerous times over a span of nearly thirty years—for *Forum*, for myself, for a book on the work of Wallace K. Harrison, the UN's *de facto* chief architect—images that I hoped would be the foundation of a comprehensive photographic library to be established by my studio.

The images accrued but never formally became the archive I had envisioned. This book is that ultimate compilation and it's gratifying to see the material presented in such a unified manner.

Introduction

Jane C. Loeffler

WHEN I FIRST visited the United Nations in 1962 it was still new and I had never seen anything like it. Soaring interior spaces, textured walls, strange abstract murals, and gifts from around the world caught my eye. I recall the amazing experience of listening to simultaneous translation through heavy headphones (who could imagine translating so fast?) and the wonder of visiting a shop filled with souvenirs from Ghana and Indonesia and other places that I knew nothing about. With brightly colored flags waving in front, it all seemed so up-beat and, well, so international. As I later learned, that was precisely the intention of those charged with the task of creating a lasting symbol of the quest for peace.

The process that produced the UN design was indeed international, but only officially peaceful. American architect Wallace K. Harrison headed a design team that included architects from eleven nations. All wanted input in every phase of planning and design. The purpose of the collaboration was to emphasize unanimity of outlook and the possibility for cooperation—even among architects whose egos were large beyond measure. It was a daunting challenge for Harrison. The fact that he pulled it off with such success was a remarkable achievement and it was rightly recognized as such in the early 1950s when the three principal buildings—the Secretariat, the Conference Building, and the General Assembly—reached completion. But the fact that critics also faulted the finished project was evidence of some discomfort with the idea of artistic compromise and architectural uncertainty about the dramatic design; it was evidence, too, of political uncertainty over the role of the UN and the very notion of international commitments.

Architectural photographer Ezra Stoller shot many of the images that made the UN memorable. Acclaimed by architects for his photographic wizardry, Stoller was already the first choice among those trying to publicize new projects when Harrison retained him to document the UN as a work in progress in 1950. Stoller returned often to the site over the following years. His widely published photographs figure prominently in UN history—a history that can be traced to the closing days of World War II.

Weary from war, representatives of the United States, the Soviet Union, the United Kingdom, and China met at Dumbarton Oaks in 1944 to commit themselves to an international organization founded to protect human rights and prevent another world war. Hopeful delegates from fifty nations signed the United Nations Charter in San Francisco on 26 June 1945. The General Assembly met for the first time in London early the next year and made the decision to locate its permanent headquarters in the United States. Three subcommittees took up the task of selecting a site and a design.

The search team established itself in New York City while considering a range of sites from Boston to Philadelphia on the East Coast and San Francisco on the West. Robert Moses, New York's parks commissioner, immediately saw the opportunity to recycle the abandoned 1939 World's Fair site at Flushing Meadows Park in Queens. He and his hastily assembled UN committee offered former fair buildings to the UN as temporary headquarters and did all they could to interest UN officials in the expansive but soggy site. Delegates arriving from around the globe, however, expressed a strong preference for a site across the East River in Manhattan.

At the same time, New York real estate speculator William Zeckendorf was busily acquiring parcels of land in Manhattan's meat-packing district between Forty-second and Forty-ninth streets along the East River, hoping to assemble enough acreage to build a sprawl-ing mixed-use development to rival Rockefeller Center (then known as Radio City). To gain insight into what made that landmark such a success, he had hired Harrison, one of Rockefeller Center's principal architects. Together, Zeckendorf and Harrison envisioned a huge development with three thirty-story apartment buildings and an array of offices, performance spaces, hotels, and parking. Raised on a platform high above First Avenue, the complex, which they dubbed "X City," echoed earlier visionary schemes, including Le Corbusier's "City of Towers," proposed in the 1920s but never realized.[1]

Harrison was a self-schooled architect who impressed clients and colleagues with his gentlemanly demeanor and his common sense. He established his own practice in 1935 after the completion of Rockefeller Center and soon won the commission to design the Theme Center for the 1939 New York World's Fair. The famed Trylon and Perisphere came to symbolize that fair, which billed itself as "The World of Tomorrow." And as Victoria Newhouse notes in her biogra-phy of Harrison, it also established his reputation as a designer will-ing to compromise to get things done.[2]

For many years Harrison worked closely with the Rockefellers. He traveled to Caracas with Nelson Rockefeller in 1940 to design the

Avila Hotel and subsequently joined Rockefeller in Washington during the war, working with him to coordinate inter-American affairs for the State Department. It is no surprise that the well-connected Harrison emerged at the center of the deal that brought the UN to its riverside site.

Realizing that he lacked concessions from the city and needed cash to move ahead with his "X City" project, Zeckendorf was ready to sell his already assembled site when UN planners focused their attention on built-up Manhattan. The Rockefellers and other city and state boosters wanted more than anything to keep the UN in New York. With Moses orchestrating behind the scenes and Harrison as the go-between, the Rockefellers purchased the "X City" site for $8.5 million and donated it to the UN late in 1946. Writing in *The Nation*, Frederick Gutheim was one of the many who strongly objected to the site—too small, he said, to accommodate the headquarters, let alone housing for an international community estimated to total 52,530 persons. He also opposed the widely-publicized idea of an international design competition, arguing that only Americans were qualified to design modern skyscrapers. With architects and editorial writers debating the pros and cons of a competition and everyone vying for a piece of the hot project, Trygve Lie, the UN's first secretary-general, turned to Harrison, the indispensable insider, and appointed him director of planning (effectively chief architect) early in 1947.[3]

Harrison took charge of the UN job and promptly put together the design team that included: G. A. Soilleux (Australia), Gaston Brunfaut (Belgium), Oscar Niemeyer (Brazil), Ernest Cormier (Canada), Ssu-ch'eng Liang (China), Le Corbusier (France), Sven Markelius (Sweden), Nikolai D. Bassov (USSR), Howard M. Robertson (United Kingdom), and Julio Vilamajo (Uruguay). Along with added advisors and consultants, this rather unwieldy assemblage met daily for months. Communicating largely through sketches, they struggled to solve the problem of representation—how to use modern architecture to convey confidence in a prosperous and peaceful future.

From the outset, the idea of a tall tower attracted the group. Although the UN might have been more accurately symbolized by its General Assembly, the meeting place for delegates from all member nations, the architects seized upon the office tower as an opportunity to realize a dream that had long captivated the profession. Mies van der Rohe had proposed a glass skyscraper in 1920 and since that time Le Corbusier had been relentlessly advocating his own ideal—a whole city of glass skyscrapers rising "like crystals, clean and transparent," each soaring above the dirt and disorder of existing cities, each surrounded by foliage and green fields, and each flooded with air and sunlight.[4] Ignoring the fact that his scheme would have created a subterranean world of darkness through which traffic would be channeled, and somehow imagining that he could eliminate congestion, pollution, and other urban ills by raising buildings on platforms and spacing them far apart, Le Corbusier was confident in the future—as long as it was designed to his specifications.

Naturally Le Corbusier saw the UN as the perfect chance to make his mark in Manhattan, a place he had earlier labeled a "catastrophe."[5] He had made no secret of his preference for a spacious suburban site, preferable no doubt, so that his proposed office tower would not be lost among the many others that lined or soon would line the closely spaced gridded streets of New York. But with the 18-acre East River site in hand, he reversed his position and declared it to be ideal. Other members of the design team had strong opinions, too, but no one arrived with such a pre-arranged agenda and such an uncompromising attitude as the representative from France.

To his credit, Harrison managed to sideline Le Corbusier's crusade to take control of the design process. It was essential that he did

Board members and consultants to the architectural planning committee meeting in New York on 18 April 1947. Front row (left to right): Ssu-ch'eng Liang (China), Oscar Niemeyer (Brazil), Nikolai Bassov (USSR), Ernest Cormier (Canada); back row: Sven Markelius (Sweden), Le Corbusier (France), Vladimir Bodiansky (France), Wallace K. Harrison (USA), G. A. Soilleux (Australia), Max Abramovitz (USA), Ernest Weismann (Yugoslavia), John Antoniades (Greece), Matthew Nowicki (Poland).

so because he and UN officials realized the symbolic importance of a shared design, and made every effort to convey the impression that the architects were working together in harmony. Through its Office of Public Information, for example, the UN circulated now famous photographs of the design team "at work." The posed photos of the architects gazing amiably at each other and at the plans and models before them were part of what architectural historian Linda Sue Phipps aptly describes as a public information campaign aimed at presenting the design "as the unanimous product of a meeting of the minds of the world's best architects." As Phipps notes further, later accounts of the design process, preoccupied as they were with issues of authorship, undermined this aspect of the campaign—to the extent that it was believable.[6]

Many hands did contribute to the design. Le Corbusier's influence was evident, but the entire design was not his. For one thing, his drawings showed buildings raised above the ground on stilts, or *pilotis*, but the team rejected this device which separates a structure from its basement and traps cold air beneath it, an impractical solution where winters are cold. For another, he had wanted to cover the tower's glass walls with a metal or concrete screen, or *brise-soleil*, for sun control, but that too was rejected as an ice hazard. The team also nixed Liang's proposal to position the tower on an east-west axis, perpendicular to the river, in keeping with Chinese tradition.[7] But other board members did make valuable contributions, and so did Harrison's partner Max Abramovitz, who served as deputy on the Board of Design, George Dudley, the board's secretary, and Hugh Ferriss, who provided renderings of the various schemes. It was indeed a cooperative effort.

Harrison presented the completed design to the General Assembly on 21 May 1947. It consisted of the three principal buildings grouped on an open plaza: a thin, glazed office slab rising thirty-nine stories (544 feet) above a low, fan-shaped assembly building and another low rectangular building containing conference rooms and dining facilities for delegates. (A fourth structure, the Dag Hammarskjöld Library, was designed and built later—in 1961—on the site of the former New York City Housing Authority Building.) The Secretariat's size alone made the tower the centerpiece. Its long sides (287 feet), which paralleled the river in an approximate north-south direction, were to be glass curtain walls. The narrow ends (72 feet) were to be covered in thin sheets of marble. The whole was described as an expression of the functionalist ideal—meeting man's needs through a rationalized geometry.

Builders began demolition and site preparation in July 1947 and started construction of the Secretariat by the fall of 1948. Even before that, some critics expressed horror at the sight of the plan. Ever ready with a quip, architect Frank Lloyd Wright called it "a super-crate,to ship a fiasco to hell." In the same vein, editors of the *Washington Star* described it as a "diabolical dream," out of touch with history and the hopes of humanity.[8] A similar critique was later rightly leveled at America's urban renewal program, which had its inception in Le Corbusier's rhetoric of removal. But for the United Nations, what could be more hopeful than newness? What could better express man's technological know-how than a spectacular eye-catcher that would forever alter the face of the New York skyline? Why not glass (if it worked)?

Architectural modernists had embraced the so-called international style precisely because it was suitably placeless and disassociated with history. It offered a sort of architectural Esperanto, a readily recognized language that they all understood. Their eagerness to equate innovation with talent and their interest in making use of every advance in technology made the glass and aluminum curtain wall inevitable. As long as builders could build them and zoning permitted them, skyscrapers were also inevitable where land was so valuable.

The Secretariat turned out to be a handsome building. Architects may have differed on its external appearance, but its job was to provide state-of-the-art offices for 2,300 people, and that it did. Even the earliest photographs, taken by Stoller in 1950, show the grandeur that Harrison and his team were able to achieve repeating a seven-window bay ten times across, thirty-nine times. After considerable research comparing the heat absorption of different glazing materials, Harrison selected a blue-green Thermopane for the operable windows. Knowing that the costly special glass was needed only on the west facade, he nonetheless used it on both sides for uniformity. Spandrels beneath the windows were made of the same glass and painted black on the inside. Mechanical floors, placed at irregular intervals, effectively broke the monotony of the glass grid. Venetian blinds provided sun-protection and added further visual variety. The narrow end walls were faced in Vermont marble, possibly selected to please former Vermont Senator Warren Austin, chairman of the Headquarters Advisory Committee and Permanent Representative of the United States to the United Nations.

Architectural Forum presented the Secretariat to its readers with a twenty-page spread in November 1950. Stoller's photographs, featured there, included a head-on view of the exterior, an angled view of the window-wall showing its fabric-like surface, views of the lobby, stairways, halls, and elevators, details of unusual light fixtures and air diffusers, and views of offices (in which the furniture now looks so much more dated than the architecture around it). Like all of the photographs he took at the UN, these earliest images were straight-forward, seemingly perfectly positioned, and uniformly sharp.

To fit the magazine format, *Forum* editors cropped the photos, often deleting foregrounds through which viewers step into two-dimensional images. By contrast, the original photographs show how Stoller carefully constructed his views using floor tiles and door frames, for instance, to organize the picture space. They also reveal telling details, some cropped out by former editors—such as the (dial) telephone, a Stoller favorite—that sits alone on a newly carpeted office floor waiting for the furniture and the people who are sure to follow (page 29).

Tucked behind the Secretariat, the Conference Building featured three meeting halls, each with an 18-foot ceiling, each overlooking the East River through a huge wall of glass, each with separate galleries for the public and the press, and each designed by a different Scandinavian architect. The Security Council is best known, perhaps, because it meets in times of crisis when peace is threatened. Norwegian architect Arnstein Arneberg designed its interior using royal blue and gold for walls and fabrics with an array of spotlights that dazzle like stars above. The room was a gift from Norway.

Swedish architect Sven Markelius designed the Economic and Social Council chamber, a gift from Sweden. The Markelius design boasted narrow pine slats that softened the rectilinear shape of the room, great round lights above, and exposed ductwork painted gray, black, and white. Danish architect Finn Juhl designed the Trusteeship Council chamber, a gift from Denmark. Its most striking features were an open dropped ceiling, louvered wooden walls, and bi-directional wall-mounted spotlights.

Stoller captured these and other features in photographs of the Conference Building, some published in *Architectural Forum* as early as April 1952 when the building was just finished. In addition to the chamber interiors, he also recorded the sweeping river panorama from the delegates' dining room, lounges furnished with built-in banquettes and Barcelona chairs, futuristic-looking escalators, and cantilevered stairs that appeared to be suspended in air. In all, the Conference Building was a showcase for modern design. In particular, Markelius's "unfinished" ceiling caused a sensation, and not just among architects.

By October 1952 the General Assembly was also complete. It showed the most visible signs of compromise because it was originally designed as a pinched rectangle with two flared ends, each end leading to a separate meeting hall. For the sake of economy, one hall was eliminated from the plan. Rather than reconfigure the exterior, Harrison only modified it slightly and used the same scheme to house a single hall. As a result, the great glazed south wall (that looks like it should be the main entrance) is no entrance at all. Visitors enter at the less inviting north end; delegates enter via ramps on the west.

Also, as Newhouse tells it, Harrison hastily added the curious dome when advised that Congress would be more likely to authorize the interest-free loan (needed to finance construction) if the building made a nod to tradition.[9]

Despite the missteps, the General Assembly, with its dynamic profile, instantly animated the trio of buildings. Not only designed as an efficient workplace for delegates, the General Assembly was also designed as a tourist attraction. Stoller's photographs, first published in the fall of 1952, showed the sweeping curves of the lobby balconies, the exposed ductwork high above, and the great glass wall at the south end. They showed, too, the cacophony of the meeting room itself with its louvered walls, glittering lights, splash-like murals, and seats arranged in great curved rows as if before a high altar. Critics such as Lewis Mumford who faulted it for resembling a theater simply missed the point that Soviet premier Nikita Khruschev made clear when he later visited the UN, pounding his shoe on the podium as he spoke.[10] The UN is indeed a setting for drama. By attracting a steady stream of tourists and allowing them to witness the day-to-day practice of international relations, the General Assembly has clearly furthered the UN's mission to build understanding. It is no accident that it resembles a world's fair theme pavilion as its purpose is so similar.

Leading architects, such as Richard Bennett, Victor Gruen, and Talbot Hamlin approved of the effort to build a modern symbol. Hamlin, for one, complimented Harrison and his colleagues for their "imaginative handling of materials." The project proved, he said, that the architects were wise to focus on creating a visually expressive experience, not just on finding a functional solution.[11] But others were less charitable. Architect Joseph Boaz called the whole thing "nothing better than embarrassing." Pietro Belluschi found the Secretariat's marble end walls "disturbing," and Richard Neutra wondered why the marble looked like galvanized steel from a distance.

Henry Hill found fault with the venetian blinds. Bruce Goff ridiculed the Secretariat as merely an office tower and deplored its "fake simplicity."[12] Pithy barbs created good magazine headlines, but such comments reflected real tensions within the profession.

Two of the issues that most challenged architects in the early 1950s were how to adapt international style architecture to disparate settings—from wintry New York to tropical Havana—and how to imbue modern architecture with meaning. No one had ready answers. When the State Department first commissioned modernists (including Harrison & Abramovitz) to design U.S. embassies abroad just after World War II, for example, the results provoked harsh criticism from members of Congress and others who saw the glass and steel structures as inappropriate. They looked like ordinary office buildings, not embassies. But no one was sure what modernist embassies were supposed to look like and modern architecture offered few devices that could convey the symbolic meaning previously produced by traditional design. Critics were disappointed by the UN for exactly the same reason—the architecture did not convey a sufficiently high public purpose. But again, who knew what that meant? The buildings proclaimed their newness for sure, but architects were searching in a modern idiom to find something more to say and apparently had not yet found it.

Some writers blamed what they saw as the flawed design on the "teamwork" approach. One architect, preferably Le Corbusier, they said, should have been responsible for the whole design. Henry-Russell Hitchcock subscribed to this belief, describing the Secretariat as "an end, not a beginning." Writing much more recently, William Curtis also expressed regret that Le Corbusier was robbed of the UN commission. The UN buildings, he said further, speak "more of the 'international hotel style' of the 1950s than they do of dignified places of assembly."[13]

Interestingly enough, Stoller's photographs of the UN capture this architectural ambivalence. His images incisively show what he saw, but they somehow seem to be searching for more. Maybe even the photographer was hoping for something more monumental?

Within the United States, political uncertainty produced added doubts about the UN. Among members of Congress and officials in the Truman and Eisenhower administrations there were many who fundamentally objected to America's rapidly rising world role. Isolationists feared foreign involvement. They furthered their ends by exploiting issues of domestic security and anxiety about communism. They labeled their foes "internationalists," and a communist conspiracy was all they could see behind the UN. To such critics, anything called the "international style" was something to avoid, not embrace. This led to unease about all architecture that claimed to be "international," and that naturally included the UN headquarters.

Despite doubts and mixed reviews, the UN design has since become an architectural icon, known and admired worldwide and illustrated with photographs in nearly every recent book on modern architecture. Visiting and revisiting the site, photographer Ezra Stoller diligently documented its evolution and created an invaluable record of a key moment in architectural history. His photographs have become icons themselves—particularly those that show the Secretariat soaring above the East River skyline (when 39 stories could still soar). They have contributed to our perception of the UN and offer us, still, one route to the world of tomorrow.

NOTES

1. Le Corbusier, *Towards a New Architecture* (1927; reprint, New York: Praeger, 1970), 54.

2. Victoria Newhouse, *Wallace K. Harrison, Architect* (New York: Rizzoli, 1989), 89.

3. Robert Caro, *The Power Broker* (New York: Alfred A. Knopf, 1974), 771–5; Frederick Gutheim, "The Last Skyscraper," *The Nation*, 28 December 1946, 755–7.

4. Le Corbusier, *When the Cathedrals Were White* (1947; reprint: New York: McGraw-Hill, 1964), 53.

5. Ibid., 36.

6. Linda Sue Phipps, "Constructing the United Nations Headquarters: Modern Architecture as Public Diplomacy" (Ph.D. diss., Harvard University, 1998), viii.

7. Newhouse, *Wallace K. Harrison*, 120.

8. "Published Comments on the United Nations Headquarters," *Journal of the American Institute of Architects* (October 1947): 158.

9. Newhouse, *Wallace K. Harrison*, 130.

10. Lewis Mumford's comments, originally published in "The Sky Line: United Nations Assembly," *The New Yorker*, 14 March 1953, 72, are reproduced in Robert A. M. Stern et. al., *New York 1960* (New York: Monacelli Press, 1997), 623.

11. Comments quoted in "The Secretariat, a Campanile, a Cliff of Glass, a Great Debate," *Architectural Forum*, (November 1950): 106–7.

12. Ibid.

13. Ibid.; William J. R. Curtis, *Modern Architecture Since 1900* (Oxford: Phaidon, 1982), 268.

Plates

PERMANENT
HEADQUARTERS
UNITED NATIONS

INFORMATION

UNITED KINGDOM
YEMEN
CUBA
CHINA
VENEZUELA
AUSTRALIA
CHILE

Drawings & Plans

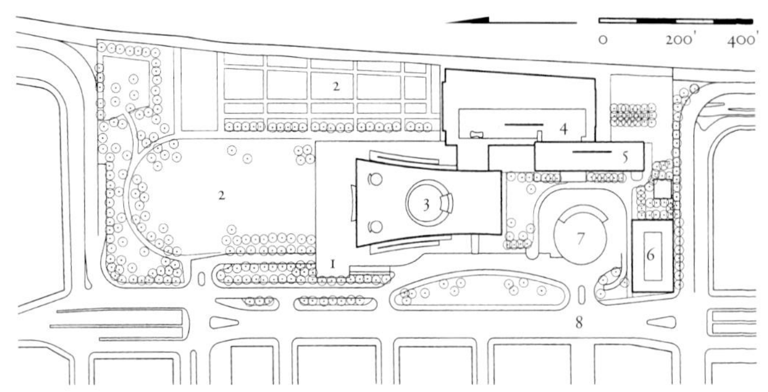

Site plan

1. VISITORS' ENTRANCE
2. GARDENS
3. GENERAL ASSEMBLY
4. CONFERENCE BUILDING
5. SECRETARIAT
6. LIBRARY
7. ROTUNDA
8. MAIN GATE

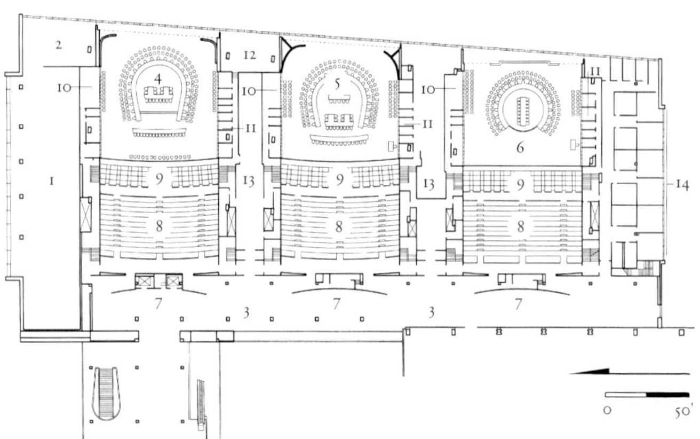

Conference Building: third floor plan

1. DELEGATE LOUNGE
2. WRITING ROOM
3. PUBLIC CORRIDOR
4. ECOSOC CHAMBER
5. TRUSTEESHIP COUNCIL CHAMBER
6. SECURITY COUNCIL CHAMBER
7. PROJECTION ROOM
8. PUBLIC SEATING
9. PRESS SEATING
10. TV & SOUND
11. TRANSLATORS
12. LOUNGE
13. FAN ROOM
14. PRESS OFFICES

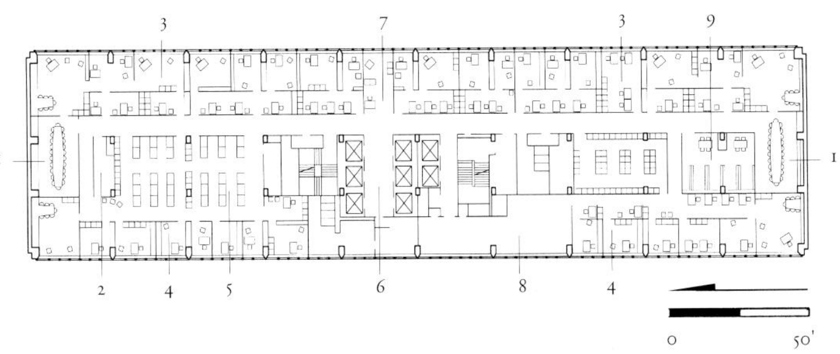

Secretariat: standard floor plan

1. CONFERENCE ROOM
2. STORAGE
3. EAST OFFICES
4. WEST OFFICES
5. TYPING POOL
6. ELEVATORS
7. RECEPTION
8. MESSENGER CENTER
9. LIBRARY

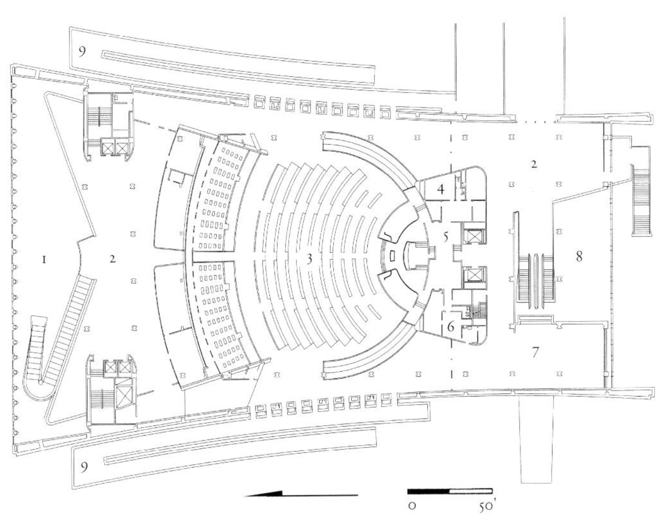

General Assembly

1. NORTH LOBBY
2. BALCONY
3. ASSEMBLY HALL
4. SECRETARY GENERAL
5. EXECUTIVE SUITE
6. PRESIDENT
7. DELEGATE LOUNGE
8. SOUTH LOBBY
9. DELEGATE ENTRANCE RAMP

Key to Photographs

FRONTISPIECE: Secretariat facade from Tudor City (1950–51)*

17 Complex from Long Island City (1950–51)

18 Secretariat with stacked pipes from the north (1950–51)

19 Site under construction (1949)

20–1 Site under construction (1949)

22 Complex under construction: view from the north (1950–51)

23 Complex under construction: view from the southwest (1950–51)

24 Secretariat from Forty-third Street (1950–51)

25 Secretariat facade (1950–51)

26 Secretariat facade under construction (1950–51)

27 Secretariat facade and temporary walkway (1950–51)

28 Secretariat lobby (1950–51)

29 Secretariat office with phone (1950–51)

30–1 Secretariat mechanical floor (1950–51)

33 View from Roosevelt Island (1977)

34 View from Long Island City (1954)

35 View from Long Island City (1954)

36 View from Roosevelt Island (1954)

37 View from the East River (1952)

38T View from the northeast (1954)

38B Gardens from Conference Building (1977)

39T View from the north (1977)

39B Gardens from Conference Building (1977)

40–1 Complex from First Avenue (1954)

42 Aerial view from the northwest (1977)

43 Secretariat entrance (1954)

44T Rotunda from the southwest (1977)

44B Rotunda from above (1954)

45T Dag Hammarskjöld Library (1977)

45B Dag Hammarskjöld Library (1977)

46–7 Secretariat lobby information desk (1954)

48 Conference Building from Secretariat lobby (1952)

49 Conference Building from the south (1952)

50 Conference Building: east facade (1954)

51 Conference Building: north facade (1977)

52–3 Conference Building: Delegates' Lounge (1977)

54–5 Conference Building: corridor to council chambers (1952)

56 Conference Building: Security Council (1953)

57T Conference Building: Trusteeship Council (1952)

57B Conference Building: Trusteeship Council (1977)

58 Conference Building: Economic and Social Council (ECOSOC), side entrance (1952)

59T Conference Building: ECOSOC (1952)

59B Conference Building: ECOSOC (1954)

61 General Assembly: view from the northwest (1977)

62 General Assembly: view from the north-west (1977)

63 General Assembly: north facade from plaza (1952)

64 Complex from the north (1977)

65 Secretariat and General Assembly ramp from the north (1977)

66 General Assembly: west facade and entrance (1952)

67 General Assembly: east facade and ramp (1952)

68 General Assembly: south facade from the west (1954)

69 General Assembly: view from Conference Building (1952)

70 General Assembly: south lobby escalator and stairs (1953)

71 General Assembly: second-story lounge (1953)

72 General Assembly: lower-level lounge (1953)

73 General Assembly: conference room (1952)

74–5 General Assembly: information desk (1952)

76 General Assembly: north lobby (1977)

77 General Assembly: north lobby (1954)

78 General Assembly: balcony above north lobby (1952)

79 General Assembly: chapel (1977)

80–1 General Assembly: view from balcony (1952)

82–3 General Assembly: assembly hall (1977)

84–5 General Assembly: assembly hall (1953)

86 General Assembly: assembly hall, view toward dais (1953)

87 General Assembly: assembly hall, delegate seating (1954)

88–9 General Assembly: assembly hall, view from dais (1953)

90 Complex at dusk from Roosevelt Island (1954)

Dates refer to the year photograph was taken. All photographs by Ezra Stoller.

Published by
Princeton Architectural Press
37 East Seventh Street
New York, NY 10003

For a catalog of books published by Princeton Architectural Press, call toll free 1.800.722.6657
or visit www.papress.com

Copyright © 1999 Princeton Architectural Press
All photographs copyright © Esto Photographics, Inc.
03 02 01 00 99   5 4 3 2 1   First Edition

No part of this book may be used or reproduced in any manner without written permission
from the publisher except in the context of reviews.

Series editor & book design: Mark Lamster
Drawings & plans: Jonah Pregerson & Mark Watanabe

Acknowledgments
I would like to thank my colleagues at Esto Photographics, especially Kent Draper and Laura
Bolli; Mary Doyle and Mike Kimines of TSI Color Lab for their help in preparing these
images; and Mark Lamster for his support from start to finish—Erica Stoller

Princeton Architectural Press acknowledges Eugenia Bell, Bernd-Christian Döll, Jane Garvie,
Caroline Green, Leslie Ann Kent, Clare Jacobson, Therese Kelly, Annie Nitschke, and Sara E.
Stemen—Kevin C. Lippert, publisher

For the licensing of Ezra Stoller images, contact Esto Photographics.
Fine art reproductions of Stoller prints are available through the James Danziger Gallery.

Printed in China

Library of Congress Cataloging-in-Publication Data

The United Nations / photographs by Ezra Stoller;
   introduction by Jane C. Loeffler. -- 1st ed.
       p.   cm. -- (The Building Blocks series)
   Includes bibliographical references.
   ISBN 1-56898-183-x (alk. paper)
   1. United Nations--Buildings--Pictorial works. 2. New York
(N.Y.)--Buildings, stru ctures, etc.--Pictorial works. 3. Harrison,
Wallace K. (Wallace Kirkman), 1895–1981--Criticism and interpretation.
   I. Stoller, Ezra. II. Series: Building Blocks series (New York, N.Y.)
NA4184.U54 1999
779'.47471--dc21   98-54868
                                              CIP